I0448786

July 2013

AMERICA COMPETES ACTS

Overall Appropriations Have Increased and Have Mainly Funded Existing Federal Research Entities

GAO Highlights

Highlights of GAO-13-612, a report to congressional committees

AMERICA COMPETES ACTS

Overall Appropriations Have Increased and Have Mainly Funded Existing Federal Research Entities

Why GAO Did This Study

Scientific and technological innovation and a workforce educated in STEM fields are critical to long-term U.S. economic competitiveness. Leaders in government, business, and education have expressed concern about the nation's ability to compete with other technologically advanced countries in these fields. In this context, Congress passed COMPETES 2007 and reauthorized the act with COMPETES 2010, each with the overall goal of investing in research and development to improve U.S. competitiveness. Among other things, the acts specifically authorized funding for certain programs.

COMPETES 2010 mandated GAO to evaluate the status of authorized programs. GAO examined (1) the extent to which funding was appropriated under the authorization of COMPETES 2007 and COMPETES 2010 and (2) what recent evaluations suggest about how programs for which the acts specifically authorized funding are working. To answer these questions, GAO reviewed relevant federal laws, interviewed agency officials, and reviewed program evaluations for quality and content.

This report contains no recommendations.

View GAO-13-612. For more information, contact Frank Rusco at (202) 512-3841 or ruscof@gao.gov.

What GAO Found

In fiscal years 2008-2012, $52.4 billion was appropriated out of the $62.2 billion authorized under the America Creating Opportunities to Meaningfully Promote Excellence in Technology, Education, and Science Act of 2007 (COMPETES 2007) and the America COMPETES Reauthorization Act of 2010 (COMPETES 2010). Almost all of these funds went to the entire budgets of three existing research entities—the National Science Foundation (NSF), the National Institute of Standards and Technology (NIST), and the Department of Energy's (DOE) Office of Science (Science)—including all of the programs and activities the entities carry out. Appropriations for NSF, NIST, and Science generally increased under the acts but did not reach levels authorized by the acts. In addition to authorizing the budgets of these entities, COMPETES 2007 and COMPETES 2010 specifically authorized funding for 40 individual programs, including some programs within and some outside of these entities. Among those 40 programs, the 12 programs that existed before COMPETES 2007 received appropriations and continue to operate. Six of 28 newly authorized programs were also funded. Of these 6 programs, 1—DOE's Advanced Research Projects Agency-Energy, set up to develop new energy technologies—is continuing operations, 3 were not funded in fiscal year 2012, and 2 were not fully implemented as of May 2013. For the 22 programs that were not funded, agency officials generally said that they did not request funding in their budget submissions; most often this was because agencies had similar programs under way or could pursue similar objectives within current programs. For example, Science said it did not request funding for the Discovery Science and Engineering Innovation Institutes because it would have duplicated other Science programs.

For the fully implemented programs for which the COMPETES Acts specifically authorized funding, recent evaluations generally reported positive results, and some evaluations provided suggestions for improvements. Recent evaluations have been conducted for almost all of the programs that were implemented, or for aspects of those programs. For example, studies of the Robert Noyce Teacher Scholarship Program found that the program has increased the number of qualified science, technology, engineering, and mathematics (STEM) teachers, but also suggested that retention of teachers in high-need schools could be improved.

Appropriations under COMPETES 2007 and COMPETES 2010 in Fiscal Years 2008-2012

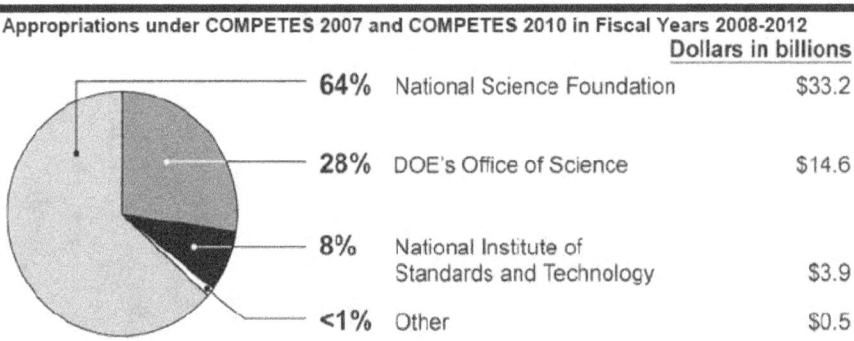

		Dollars in billions
64%	National Science Foundation	$33.2
28%	DOE's Office of Science	$14.6
8%	National Institute of Standards and Technology	$3.9
<1%	Other	$0.5

Sources: GAO analysis of data from Congresssional Research Service reports and relevant federal agencies.

Note: Because of rounding, percentages do not add to 100, and dollars do not add to $52.4 billion.

_____ **United States Government Accountability Office**

Contents

Abbreviations

ARPA-E	Advanced Research Projects Agency-Energy
Commerce	Department of Commerce
COMPETES 2007	America Creating Opportunities to Meaningfully Promote Excellence in Technology, Education, and Science Act of 2007
COMPETES 2010	America COMPETES Reauthorization Act of 2010
COMPETES Acts	COMPETES 2007 and COMPETES 2010
DOE	Department of Energy
Education	Department of Education
IGERT	Integrative Graduate Education and Research Traineeship
MEP	Hollings Manufacturing Extension Partnership
NIST	National Institute of Standards and Technology
Noyce	Robert Noyce Teacher Scholarship Program
NSF	National Science Foundation
Recovery Act	American Recovery and Reinvestment Act of 2009
REU	Research Experiences for Undergraduates
RIP	Regional Innovation Program
Science	Office of Science
STEM	Science, Technology, Engineering, and Mathematics

July 19, 2013

The Honorable John D. Rockefeller
Chairman
The Honorable John Thune
Ranking Member
Committee on Commerce, Science, and Transportation
United States Senate

The Honorable Lamar Smith
Chairman
The Honorable Eddie Bernice Johnson
Ranking Member
Committee on Science, Space, and Technology
House of Representatives

Scientific and technological innovation and a workforce educated in the fields of science, technology, engineering, and mathematics (STEM) are critical to long-term U.S. economic competitiveness. In recent years, leaders in government, business, and education have expressed concern that declines in federal funding for scientific research, coupled with a shortage of qualified students and future workers in STEM fields, threaten the nation's ability to compete with other technologically advanced countries. For example, according to a group of leaders gathered by the National Academies in 2005 and 2010 to examine U.S. competitiveness in the twenty-first century, scientific research and education are necessary investments that will drive the economy and allow the United States to maintain the economic strength to provide services such as health care and national security in the current economic and fiscal climate.[1]

For decades, the federal government has invested in scientific research at a number of agencies and departments, including the National Science

---

[1]The National Academies comprises four organizations: the National Academy of Sciences, National Academy of Engineering, Institute of Medicine, and National Research Council. The group gathered in 2010 was made up of members of the committee that wrote the 2007 National Academies report *Rising above the Gathering Storm: Energizing and Employing America for a Brighter Economic Future*, which made recommendations to ensure the United States maintains its leadership in science and engineering.

Foundation (NSF), the Department of Energy (DOE), and the Department of Commerce's (Commerce) National Institute of Standards and Technology (NIST). The federal government also invests in STEM education through the Department of Education (Education), NSF, DOE, and other departments.

Congress passed the America Creating Opportunities to Meaningfully Promote Excellence in Technology, Education, and Science Act of 2007 (COMPETES 2007)[2] with the overall goal of investing in research and development to improve U.S. competitiveness. The act also authorized investments in education in STEM fields. In 2011, Congress passed the COMPETES Reauthorization Act of 2010 (COMPETES 2010).[3] Together, these acts authorized $62.2 billion in funding from fiscal year 2008 through 2012. For fiscal year 2013, COMPETES 2010 authorized an additional $16 billion, bringing the total amount authorized under the acts to $78.2 billion. Both COMPETES 2007 and COMPETES 2010 (COMPETES Acts) authorized the entire budgets of three previously existing federal research entities: NSF, DOE's Office of Science (Science), and NIST, including all activities and the many programs within these entities. In addition, the acts specifically authorized funding for 40 individual programs, including some programs within and some outside of NSF, Science, and NIST.

COMPETES 2010 directed us to evaluate the status of programs authorized under the act, including the extent to which those programs have been funded, implemented, and are contributing to achieving the goals of the act. In response, we (1) determined the extent to which funding was appropriated under the authorization of the COMPETES Acts and (2) examined what recent evaluations suggest about how implemented programs for which the acts specifically authorized funding are working.

To conduct this work, we reviewed relevant laws and program evaluations, and we interviewed agency officials from Commerce, including NIST and the Economic Development Administration; Education; DOE, including Science and the Advanced Research Projects

---

[2]Pub. L. No. 110-69, 121 Stat. 572 (Aug. 9, 2007).

[3]Pub. L. No. 111-358, 124 Stat. 3982 (Jan. 4, 2011).

Agency–Energy;[4] and NSF. To identify the entities and programs for which the COMPETES Acts specifically authorized funding, we reviewed the COMPETES Acts. To determine the extent to which funding was appropriated to such entities and programs, we reviewed appropriations data in Congressional Research Service reports and agency budget justification documents, and we confirmed these data with agency officials. Agency officials were not able to provide complete appropriations data at the program level or final appropriations data for fiscal year 2013. We also interviewed agency officials to learn about program implementation. To examine, for the implemented programs for which the COMPETES Acts specifically authorized funding, what recent evaluations suggest about how the programs are working, we reviewed evaluations published from 2008 through 2012 that were identified by agencies and through a literature review; in some cases, these studies included data on program activities that occurred before 2008. We reviewed the methodology of the identified evaluations, and we reported on the results of those we determined to be methodologically sound. (See app. I for further details on our scope and methodology.)

We conducted this performance audit from October 2012 to July 2013 in accordance with generally accepted government auditing standards. Those standards require that we plan and perform the audit to obtain sufficient, appropriate evidence to provide a reasonable basis for our findings and conclusions based on our audit objectives. We believe that the evidence obtained provides a reasonable basis for our findings and conclusions based on our audit objectives.

Background

In response to a congressional request in 2005, the National Academies gathered a group of business, government, and academic leaders to identify steps the leaders thought would ensure that the United States is a leader in science and engineering and can compete, prosper, and be secure in the twenty-first century. The resulting 2007 report, entitled *Rising above the Gathering Storm: Energizing and Employing America for a Brighter Economic Future*, recommended a number of specific actions

---

[4]For the purposes of this report, we are considering Advanced Research Projects Agency–Energy to be a program.

to address these goals.[5] Among other things, the report advocated increasing federal investment in long-term basic and cross-disciplinary scientific research, creating an agency within DOE to support transformational energy research that might be high risk but could also provide dramatic benefits for the nation, increasing the number and skills of science and mathematics teachers in primary and secondary schools, and investing in higher education with the goal of increasing the number of undergraduate and graduate students with degrees in science, engineering, and mathematics fields. The COMPETES Acts addressed some of the actions in these areas. For example, COMPETES 2007 authorized creation of the Advanced Research Projects Agency-Energy in DOE to overcome long-term and high-risk technological barriers in developing energy technologies, and it authorized programs in Education and NSF to train teachers in STEM fields.

Investments in scientific research have led to significant advances such as the development of the Internet, satellites, aircraft, and the mapping of the human genome, while investments in STEM education have provided multiple forms of support for developing a highly qualified STEM workforce. However, evaluations of such investments face inherent challenges, such as those related to the long-term nature of many scientific research projects, an inability to predict certain outcomes, and difficulty tying specific investments to direct outcomes. As we reported in 2012, evaluations of STEM education programs may be hindered by inconsistent collection of output data, such as the number of institutions or students directly served by programs.[6] Further, efforts to evaluate the effectiveness of investments in scientific research and STEM education in improving U.S. competitiveness—the overall goal of the COMPETES Acts—are complicated by a number of factors. For example, it is difficult to measure competitiveness. The Council on Competitiveness, a group of business, academic, and labor leaders focused on ensuring U.S. prosperity, reported that traditional measures of competitiveness, such as trade balances, levels of foreign direct investment, employment, or wages

---

[5]National Academy of Sciences, National Academy of Engineering, and Institute of Medicine of the National Academies. *Rising above the Gathering Storm: Energizing and Employing America for a Brighter Economic Future.* (Washington, D.C.: National Academies Press, 2007).

[6]GAO, *Science, Technology, Engineering, and Mathematics Education: Strategic Planning Needed to Better Manage Overlapping Programs Across Multiple Agencies*, GAO-12-108 (Washington, D.C.: Jan. 20, 2012).

may not fully capture a nation's competitiveness because of the complexities brought about by multinational corporations competing in constantly shifting global networks. Further, complications arise from ambiguities surrounding the term competitiveness, which has multiple definitions.

Efforts are under way to address some of these challenges. For example, STAR Metrics—Science and Technology for America's Reinvestment: Measuring the Effect of Research on Innovation, Competitiveness, and Science—is a partnership between science agencies and research institutions to consistently document the outcomes of federally funded science investments. In addition, the National Science and Technology Committee on STEM Education within the Office of Science and Technology Policy collects and maintains information on how investments in STEM education are distributed across agencies, programs, and target groups. The committee compiled a comprehensive inventory of STEM education programs across the federal government in 2011 and released a 5-year federal STEM education plan in May 2013 to establish a strategy for focusing federal STEM education investments so they have the most significant impact possible on national priorities.

As we reported in 2010 when we reviewed COMPETES 2007, agencies collect data and use different approaches to evaluate their progress toward long-term outcomes.[7] NSF, DOE, Commerce, and Education use several tools—which may either broadly assess agency-wide activities or focus on program-level activities—to evaluate their scientific research and STEM education activities. Such tools include the following:

- advisory committees, such as NSF's committees that exist for each directorate—for example, the Education and Human Resources Advisory Committee provides advice, guidance, and recommendations concerning NSF's science and engineering education programs;

- performance reviews, such as Commerce's Annual Performance and Accountability Reports, which provide data on performance measures for NIST including the number of publications produced, or the

[7]GAO, *America COMPETES Act: It Is Too Early to Evaluate Programs Long-Term Effectiveness, but Agencies Could Improve Reporting of High-Risk, High-Reward Research Priorities*, GAO-11-127R (Washington, D.C.: Oct. 7, 2010).

Advanced Research Projects Agency–Energy's (ARPA-E) quarterly technical milestone reviews of funded projects, which help reviewers decide if project funding should be continued;

- Committees of Visitors, such as those used by NSF, Science and NIST, which are groups of external experts that assess the overall quality of program operations and, in some cases, program outcomes; and

- formal program evaluations, which are systematic, empirical studies used by agencies to assess how well a particular program or component of a program is working.

Appropriations Generally Increased but Fell Short of Authorizations, and Most Newly Authorized Programs Were Not Funded

Of the $62.2 billion authorized under the COMPETES Acts in fiscal years 2008 through 2012, $52.4 billion was appropriated, including $51.9 billion for the entire budgets of NSF, Science, and NIST. Funding for these three entities accounts for more than 99 percent of the funding appropriated under the COMPETES Acts during this period. (See fig. 1.)

Figure 1: Appropriations under the COMPETES Acts in Fiscal Years 2008 through 2012

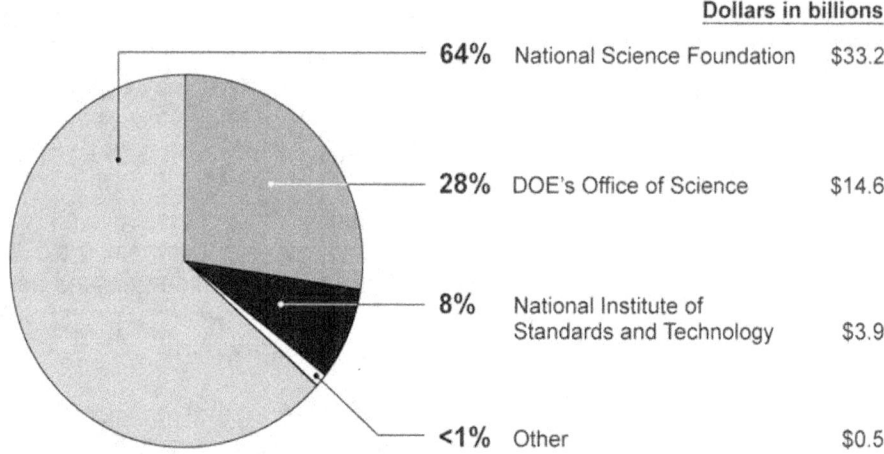

Dollars in billions

- 64% National Science Foundation $33.2
- 28% DOE's Office of Science $14.6
- 8% National Institute of Standards and Technology $3.9
- <1% Other $0.5

Sources: GAO analysis of data from Congresssional Research Service reports and relevant federal agencies.

Note: Because of rounding, percentages do not add to 100, and dollars do not add to $52.4 billion.

Appropriations for NSF, Science, and NIST generally increased in fiscal years 2008 through 2012 but did not reach authorized levels. For example, NSF's appropriations increased from about $5.9 billion in fiscal year 2007—the last year before its appropriation was authorized under the COMPETES Acts—to about $7 billion in fiscal year 2012, when it was authorized to receive $7.8 billion. Appropriations for Science, which were authorized under the COMPETES Acts starting in fiscal year 2010,[8] increased from $4.8 billion in fiscal year 2009 to about $4.9 billion in fiscal year 2012, when Science was authorized to receive $5.6 billion. Likewise, funding for NIST increased but not to authorized levels: in fiscal year 2007, before its appropriation was authorized under the COMPETES Acts, it received about $680 million, compared with $750 million in fiscal year 2012, when NIST was authorized to receive about $970 million. In addition, the American Recovery and Reinvestment Act of 2009 (Recovery Act) appropriated about $5.2 billion to these entities in fiscal year 2009. The majority of the Recovery Act appropriations—over $3 billion—went to NSF. Figure 2 shows the amounts authorized under the COMPETES Acts for NSF, Science, and NIST, as compared with the amounts appropriated, including Recovery Act appropriations.

---

[8]Appropriations for Science were authorized under the Energy Policy Act of 2005 for fiscal years 2007-2009.

Figure 2: Authorizations and Appropriations under the COMPETES Acts for NSF, DOE's Office of Science, and NIST, Fiscal Years 2008 through 2013

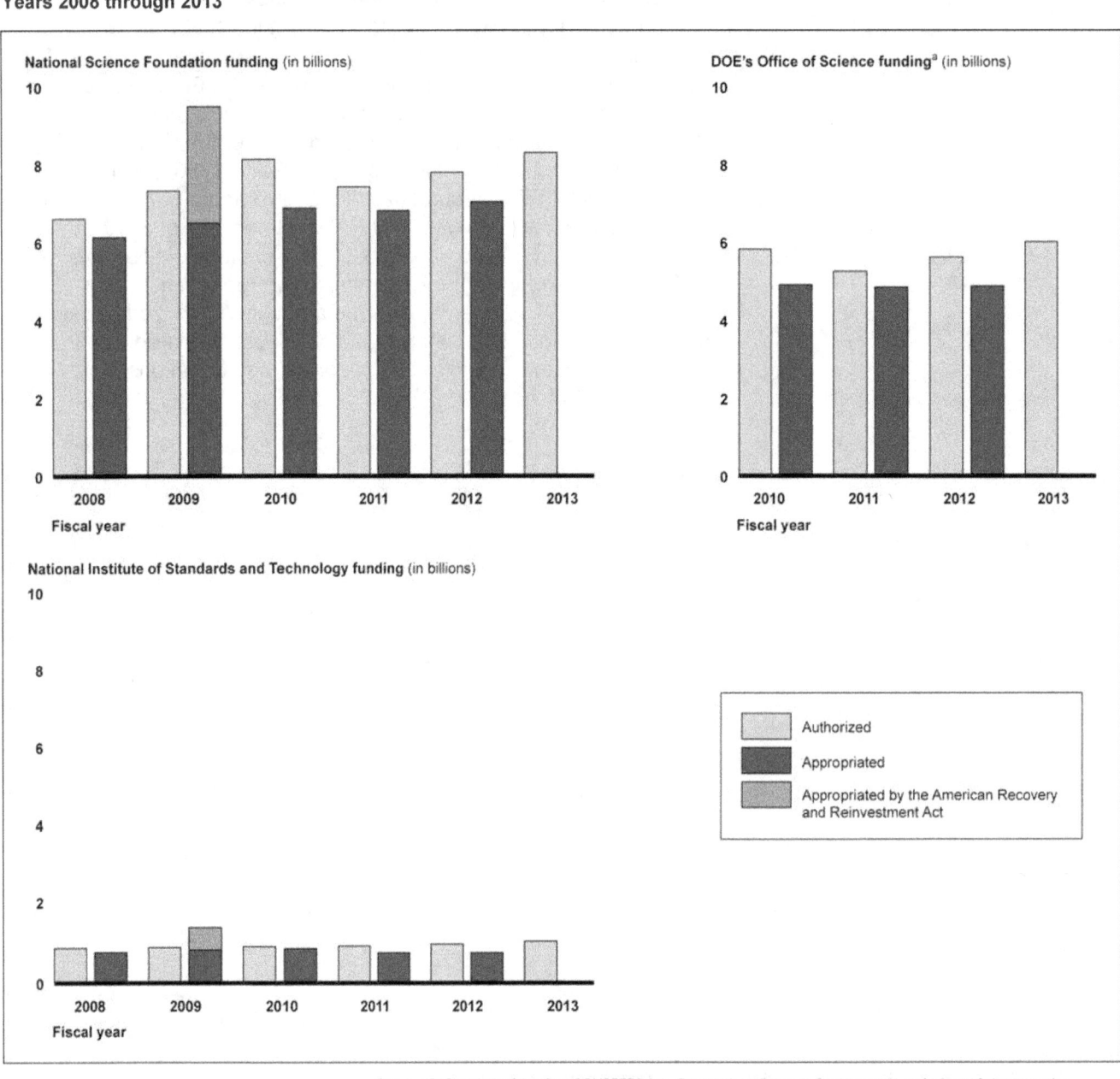

Sources: GAO analysis of data from COMPETES Acts, Congressional Research Service reports, and relevant federal agencies.

Note: As of May 2013, complete appropriations data are not available for fiscal year 2013.

[a]Funding for DOE's Office of Science was authorized under the Energy Policy Act of 2005 for fiscal years 2008 and 2009. It was authorized to receive $4.6 billion in fiscal year 2008 and $5.2 billion in fiscal year 2009. $4.0 billion was appropriated in fiscal year 2008, and $4.8 billion was appropriated in fiscal year 2009. In addition, the Office of Science received $1.6 billion under the American Recovery and Reinvestment Act in 2009.

The COMPETES Acts also specifically authorized funding for 40 individual programs, including some programs within and some outside of NSF, Science, and NIST. (See app. II.) For example, in addition to authorizing $22.1 billion for the entire budget of NSF in fiscal years 2008 through 2010, COMPETES 2007 specifically authorized $345 million of that total for NSF's Robert Noyce Teacher Scholarship Program in fiscal years 2008 through 2010. The programs not within NSF, Science, or NIST fell elsewhere within the Departments of Commerce and Energy, or in Education.

Among the 40 programs for which the COMPETES Acts specifically authorized funding, the 12 programs that existed before the acts all received appropriations and continue to operate.[9] Six of the 28 newly authorized programs also received appropriations. Of these 6 programs, 1—ARPA-E—is continuing operations, 3 did not receive appropriations in fiscal year 2012, and 2 are in the process of being implemented as of May 2013. More specifically, according to officials NSF's Science Master's Program, NIST's Technology Innovation Program, and Education's Teachers for a Competitive Tomorrow did not receive appropriations in fiscal year 2012. Officials told us the Science Master's Program and the Technology Innovation Program are in the process of shutting down, and Teachers for a Competitive Tomorrow has not awarded new grants since fiscal year 2010. Further, Commerce's Loan Guarantees for Science Park Infrastructure and Federal Loan Guarantees for Innovative Technologies in Manufacturing are in the process of being implemented, according to Commerce officials;[10] these programs first received appropriations in fiscal year 2012. Twenty-two of the 28 newly

---

[9]NIST's previously existing Baldrige Performance Excellence Program received appropriations in fiscal year 2011, but it did not receive appropriations in fiscal year 2012. It remains authorized to receive funding and is currently operating using private funds, according to agency officials.

[10]Commerce officials noted that it can take years to implement loan guarantee programs. They expect the Loan Guarantees for Innovative Technologies in Manufacturing program to issue its first loans in late 2014 or early or mid-2015. The Loan Guarantees for Science Park Infrastructure program is in an earlier stage of implementation; Officials did not yet have a timeline for issuing loans under this program.

authorized programs did not receive appropriations, including 9 programs that were newly authorized in COMPETES 2007 but repealed in COMPETES 2010.

In total, 16 of the 40 programs for which the COMPETES Acts specifically authorized funding have been implemented, including the 12 previously existing programs, ARPA-E, and the 3 newly authorized programs that did not receive appropriations in fiscal year 2012. As noted previously, two other newly authorized programs that received appropriations are in the process of being implemented. As shown in figure 3, the implemented programs generally focus on five areas: (1) research and development programs focus on activities aimed at enhancing scientific research and development,(2) manufacturing performance programs focus on supporting innovation among U.S. manufacturers and other organizations,(3) STEM teacher training programs focus on education and professional development for prospective or existing STEM teachers, (4) STEM undergraduate programs focus on encouraging or improving undergraduate STEM education, and (5) STEM graduate programs focus on supporting graduate students training for careers in research or education in STEM disciplines.

Figure 3: Implemented Programs for Which the COMPETES Acts Specifically Authorized Funding, by Focus Area and Agency

	Implemented programs	Research and development	Manufacturing performance	STEM[a] teacher training	STEM undergraduate	STEM graduate	Program descriptions
Commerce — NIST[b]	Baldrige Performance Excellence Program[c]		●				Aims to improve the performance of U.S. organizations by developing evaluation criteria and sharing performance strategies
	Hollings Manufacturing Extension Partnership		●				Provides innovation and process improvement services to small and midsize U.S. manufacturers
	Technology Innovation Program		●				Supports high-risk, high-reward research for critical needs in civil infrastructure and manufacturing
Education	Teachers for a Competitive Tomorrow (bachelor's and master's programs)			●			Enables grantees (colleges and universities) to develop and implement programs providing courses of study that integrate teacher education with STEM fields or critical foreign languages
Energy	Advanced Research Projects Agency–Energy	●					Advances high-potential, high-impact energy technologies by providing researchers with funding and technical assistance
National Science Foundation (NSF)	Advanced Technological Education				●		Focuses on the education of technicians for high-technology fields
	Experimental Program to Stimulate Competitive Research	●					Supports improvements in the research and development capacity of participating states to advance their science and engineering capabilities
	Faculty Early Career Development Program	●					Supports junior faculty who exhibit leadership in integrating research and education
	Graduate Research Fellowship Program					●	Supports outstanding graduate students in NSF-supported STEM disciplines who are pursuing research-based master's and doctoral degrees
	Integrative Graduate Education and Research Traineeship					●	Supports the graduate education of U.S. scientists and engineers who will pursue careers in research and education
	Major Research Instrumentation Program	●					Supports the development and acquisition of major state-of-the-art instrumentation, thereby building institutional capacity to train a diverse workforce in environments that integrate research and education
	Math and Science Education Partnerships			●			Awards grants to partnerships or teams of institutions of higher education and K-12 school systems to increase the number and quality of STEM teachers, especially in underserved areas
	Research Experiences for Undergraduates				●		Supports active research participation by undergraduate students
	Robert Noyce Teacher Scholarship Program			●			Encourages talented STEM students and professionals to pursue teaching careers in elementary and secondary schools
	Science Master's Program					●	Prepares graduate students for careers by providing them with a strong foundation in STEM disciplines
	STEM Talent Expansion Program				●		Seeks to increase the number of students receiving degrees in established or emerging STEM fields

☐ Subagency or office   ☐ Program did not receive appropriations in fiscal year 2012

Sources: GAO analysis of program information from relevant federal agencies.

Notes: The focus areas identified are not mutually exclusive and programs may be engaged in activities across multiple focus areas.

Two other programs that received appropriations—Commerce's Loan Guarantees for Science Park Infrastructure and Federal Loan Guarantees for Innovative Technologies in Manufacturing—have not yet been implemented as of May 2013.

[a]STEM refers to Science, Technology, Engineering, and Mathematics.

[b]NIST refers to National Institutes of Standards and Technology.

[c]The Baldrige Performance Excellence Program did not receive federal funding in 2012, but it continues to operate with private funding.

With few exceptions, agency officials told us they did not include funding requests in their budget submissions for the programs that did not receive funding. Agencies did include funding requests in their budget submissions for 4 of the 22 newly authorized programs that did not receive funding. Specifically, Education requested appropriations for the Math Now program in fiscal years 2008 and 2009 and for the Foreign Language Partnership and Advanced Placement and International Baccalaureate programs in fiscal year 2009, while Commerce requested appropriations in fiscal year 2012 for the Regional Innovation Program. For the other 18 programs, officials most often told us they did not request appropriations because their agencies already had similar programs under way or could work within current programs to carry out similar activities. For example, Science officials told us the office did not request appropriations for the Discovery Science and Engineering Innovation Institutes because the program's implementation would have duplicated existing activities. Commerce officials told us that the department's Economic Development Administration implemented certain aspects of the Regional Innovation Program (RIP) through the existing Economic Adjustment Assistance program when RIP did not receive appropriations. However, the officials also noted that by implementing aspects of RIP in this manner they have reduced funding available to other worthwhile aspects of the Economic Adjustment Assistance program. In other cases, officials told us they did not request appropriations because the programs did not fit into the agency mission or because the agencies prioritized other programs in light of limited resources or other factors.

Recent Evaluations Generally Suggest Positive Results and Some Recommend Improvements for Implemented Programs

Recent evaluations that we identified have generally suggested positive results for the fully implemented programs for which the COMPETES Acts specifically authorized funding; some of the evaluations have also recommended ways to improve the programs. Recent evaluations have been conducted for 15 of 16 fully implemented programs.[11] According to NSF officials, no evaluation of the Science Master's Program was published during 2008-2012, which is the time frame of evaluations included in our review. These evaluations have provided information on how well programs—or aspects of programs—were working in each of the five areas on which the programs focus. Many studies have also made recommendations for program improvement. Following are examples of selected evaluations and key findings for programs in the five focus areas:[12]

- *Research and development.* Studies for these programs found that they were generally producing positive results and noted areas for continued improvement. For example, one study used econometric modeling to examine the effects of the Experimental Program to Stimulate Competitive Research, which aims to improve the research and development capacity of participating states.[13] The results suggested participating states have been effective in growing federal financial support for science and engineering at a faster rate compared with nonparticipating states. However, the authors noted that while the effect they found was statistically significant, it was a small effect. They concluded that more enhanced and innovative efforts are needed to sustainably build states' research and development capacity. In another example, our 2012 review of ARPA-E found that it successfully funded projects that would not have been funded solely by private investors, in keeping with its goals.[14]

---

[11]Our review included findings from 21 studies, including Committee of Visitors reports, covering 13 programs. See appendix I for information on how we identified studies for this report.

[12]See appendix I for information on how we selected evaluation examples. Many of these evaluations reported a number of findings. We reported what we considered to be the evaluations' main findings.

[13]Yonghong Wu, "Tackling Undue Concentration of Federal Research Funding: An Empirical Assessment on NSF's Experimental Program to Stimulate Competitive Research (EPSCoR)," *Research Policy* 39 (2010): 835-841.

[14]GAO, *Department of Energy: Advanced Research Projects Agency-Energy Could Benefit from Information on Applicants' Prior Funding*, GAO-12-112 (Washington, D.C.: Jan. 13, 2012).

Separately, the DOE Inspector General recommended that ARPA-E improve by establishing a systematic approach to meeting its technology transfer and outreach requirements.[15]

- *Manufacturing performance.* Among the three implemented programs in this focus area for which the COMPETES Acts specifically authorized funding, only the Hollings Manufacturing Extension Partnership program (MEP) continued to receive federal funding as of May 2013. MEP provides services to small and midsize U.S. manufacturers to help them innovate and improve their processes. A survey of MEP clients found that, for some clients, the program was successful in generating positive results measured in terms of sales, investment levels, cost savings, and jobs created or retained.[16] Another study of this program concluded, on the basis of a range of methodologies including focus groups and interviews, that program changes over time could better position MEP to respond to challenges facing the manufacturing sector.[17] For example, the study suggested that MEP expand its reach to a larger number of clients. Specifically, the study noted that working in-depth with 30,000 firms would allow MEP to have a substantially greater impact on the manufacturing sector. The study authors also stated that MEP would need resources to expand to the recommended scale.

- *STEM teacher training.* Studies for programs in this focus area found that the programs produced positive outcomes but also identified areas requiring attention. One program—the Robert Noyce Teacher Scholarship Program (Noyce)—aims to encourage talented STEM students and professionals to pursue teaching careers in elementary

---

[15]Department of Energy Office of Inspector General, *Audit Report: The Advanced Research Projects Agency – Energy*, OAS-RA-11-11 (Washington, D.C.: Aug. 22, 2011). ARPA-E is required to undergo a comprehensive evaluation of its activities in 2015, after it has been in operation for 6 years.

[16]Manufacturing Extension Partnership, *Delivering Measurable Results to Manufacturing Clients: Fiscal Year 2009 Results* (Washington, D.C.: March, 2011). These findings were based on MEP surveys of program clients; fewer than 50 percent of respondents reported that MEP had an impact on sales, investment levels, jobs created, or jobs retained. A majority of client respondents did report cost savings in areas such as labor, materials, inventory, and energy.

[17]Stone & Associates and the Center for Regional Economic Competitiveness , *Re-examining the Manufacturing Extension Partnership Business Model: Alternatives for Increasing the Program's Impact on US Manufacturing Sector Performance* (study prepared for the NIST Manufacturing Extension Partnership, McLean, VA, October 2010).

GAO-13-612 America COMPETES Acts

and secondary schools, including high-need schools. An evaluation team at the University of Minnesota conducted a multiyear evaluation of Noyce that included data from 2003 through 2007 and used a mixed-method design to address a number of evaluation questions.[18] The study concluded, among other findings, that Noyce was accomplishing its goal of producing STEM teachers. A Committee of Visitors review of Noyce examined a random sample of funding awards and other program actions to assess the quality of the program's merit review process and overall management.[19] This review was generally positive; however, the committee noted that approximately two-thirds of Noyce scholars left their school assignments after their service commitment and, while some left high-need schools for other schools, others left teaching altogether. The University of Minnesota study also addressed teacher retention and developed a qualitative model identifying several characteristics that appeared to predict teacher retention.[20] The findings from this analysis suggested, for example, that community and location considerations—such as proximity to family and friends and distance between home and work—played an important role in scholars' decisions to stay in or leave high-need schools. Based on this finding, the authors suggested Noyce could investigate recruiting and selecting candidates that reside near communities with high-need schools to potentially improve retention.

- *STEM undergraduate.* Studies of programs in this focus area found that program portfolios were contributing to stated goals, such as integrating research with education, but could be improved. For example, Research Experiences for Undergraduates (REU) aims to support active research participation by undergraduate students by providing grants for educational institutions to initiate and conduct projects that engage a number of students in research. Two studies

---

[18]Frances Lawrenz et al., *University of Minnesota Evaluation of the Robert Noyce Teacher Scholarship Program: Final Summary Report* (Minneapolis, MN: August 2009).

[19]National Science Foundation Committee of Visitors, *Fiscal Year 2011 Report Template for NSF Committee of Visitors: Robert Noyce Teacher Scholarship Program* (Washington, D.C.: October 31-November 1, 2011).

[20]Allison Kirchhoff et al., *University of Minnesota Evaluation of the Robert Noyce Teacher Scholarship Program, Final Report Section Six: A Model of the Pathway to Retention in High Need Settings, Analysis of the Noyce Scholar Interviews* (Minneapolis, MN: May 2009).

have been conducted to gather in-depth information about the activities, outcomes, and impacts of REU awards from the perspectives of former REU students and participating faculty members. An initial survey of participants and faculty members covered awards granted from fiscal year 2003 through 2006.[21] The results suggested that participating in a wide variety of research activities was the best predictor for increasing participants' awareness, confidence, skills, and understanding of research concepts and methods. A second survey followed-up with students who responded to the initial survey and sought to measure the longer-term impacts of REU and other research experiences.[22] On the basis of the survey results, the authors concluded that participating in undergraduate research has resulted in more students deciding to go to graduate school or to consider a career in research. In addition to other findings, the study noted that respondents benefitted from their undergraduate research experiences, and it also suggested improvement in many areas.

- *STEM graduate.* Studies of programs with this focus area noted that programs were addressing agency or national priorities and pointed out areas for improvement. For example, Integrative Graduate Education and Research Traineeship (IGERT) supports the education of U.S. scientists and engineers who will pursue careers in research and education. The seamless integration of research and education is a high priority for NSF. A 2011 evaluation of IGERT used two approaches: a descriptive component that included a survey of all PhD graduates as of 2007 who had received IGERT funding, and a quasi-experimental comparison of IGERT PhD graduates with comparable non-IGERT graduates.[23] The survey results indicated that more than 800 students had graduated and entered the workforce and that most of these graduates (96 percent) reported that their IGERT

---

[21]Mary P. Hancock and Susan H. Russell, *Research Experiences for Undergraduates (REU) in the Directorate for Engineering (ENG): 2003-2006 Participant Survey* (Menlo Park, CA: August 2008).

[22]Lori Thurgood, Christopher Ordowich, and Prudy Brown, *Research Experiences for Undergraduates (REU) in the Directorate for Engineering (ENG): Follow-Up of FY2006 Student Participants* (Menlo Park, CA: October 2010).

[23]Jennifer Carney et al., *Evaluation of the National Science Foundation's Integrative Graduate Education and Research Traineeship Program (IGERT): Follow-Up Study of IGERT Graduates* (Arlington, VA: February 2011).

experience positively contributed to their ability to finish their PhDs. A majority of respondents (94 percent) also reported that the IGERT experience helped them obtain their current work positions. An exploratory analysis comparing IGERT graduates with non-IGERT graduates from similar academic departments found no significant difference between the graduates in securing employment, but they did find that IGERT graduates reported a greater interest in interdisciplinary education or research training.

Agency Comments and Our Evaluation

We provided a draft of this report to Commerce, DOE, Education, and NSF for comment. Commerce's Economic Development Administration did not have any comments on the draft. Commerce's NIST provided written comments, which are reproduced in appendix III, along with our response. On behalf of NIST, the Secretary of Commerce stated that the draft, as scoped, does not fully capture the significant positive impact that the COMPETES Acts have had on NIST. As noted in our response in appendix III, the scope of our review is based on a mandate in COMPETES 2010 that calls for GAO to evaluate the extent to which programs authorized under the law have been funded, implemented, and are contributing to achieving the goals of the act. Our report addresses the total appropriations to NIST in fiscal years 2008 through 2012 in objective 1. To satisfy the needs of our congressional clients, we focused our review on programs for which the COMPETES Acts specifically authorized funding. DOE provided technical comments, which we incorporated as appropriate. Education did not have any comments on the draft. NSF provided technical comments, which we incorporated, as appropriate.

We are sending copies of this report to the Secretaries of Commerce, Education, and Energy; the Director of NSF; the appropriate congressional committees; and other interested parties. In addition, the report is available at no charge on the GAO website at http://www.gao.gov.

If you or your staff members have any questions about this report, please contact me at (202) 512-3841 or ruscof@gao.gov. Contact points for our Offices of Congressional Relations and Public Affairs may be found on the last page of this report. GAO staff who made key contributions to this report are listed in appendix IV.

Frank Rusco
Director, Natural Resources and Environment

Appendix I: Scope and Methodology

To inform our objectives, we reviewed our October 2010 report on agency obligations under the America Creating Opportunities to Meaningfully Promote Excellence in Technology, Education, and Science Act of 2007 (COMPETES 2007) and the steps agencies were taking to evaluate implemented programs under COMPETES 2007.[1] We also reviewed relevant laws, including COMPETES 2007 and the COMPETES Reauthorization Act of 2010 (COMPETES 2010), and we interviewed agency officials from the National Science Foundation (NSF); the Department of Energy (DOE), including the Office of Science (Science) and the Advanced Research Projects Agency–Energy (ARPA-E); the Department of Commerce (Commerce), including the National Institute of Standards and Technology (NIST) and the Economic Development Administration; and the Department of Education (Education).

To determine the extent to which funding was appropriated under the authorization of the COMPETES Acts, we reviewed the laws and identified the entities and programs for which the acts specifically authorized funding. To determine the extent to which funding was actually provided to such entities and programs, we reviewed annual appropriations data in Congressional Research Service reports and agency budget justification documents, and confirmed these data with agency officials. Agency officials were not able to provide complete appropriations data at the program level. Complete final appropriations data for fiscal year 2013 were also not available. We interviewed agency officials to learn about the status of programs that received funding. We also asked agency officials which programs were included in annual budget requests and why other programs were not included in those requests.

To examine what the results of evaluations suggest about how the programs for which the COMPETES Acts specifically authorized funding are working, we identified and reviewed a selection of recent studies that evaluated these programs. To identify these evaluations, we conducted a literature review and interviewed agency officials. Specifically, we conducted a literature search in databases such as ProQuest, SciSearch, and Academic One to search for recent reports or publications that evaluated programs authorized by the COMPETES Acts. We conducted an initial review of the summaries of the reports or publications returned

---

[1]GAO-11-127R.

in our literature search and provided by agencies, and we excluded those that did not appear to evaluate how well programs were working and were not published in 2008-2012.[2] We included studies published from 2008 through 2012; in some cases, these studies included data on program activities that occurred before 2008. We reviewed the methodology of the identified studies and reported on the results of those we determined to be methodologically sound and reliable for the purposes of our report. We included the results of 21 studies covering 13 programs in our review. We reported findings on a select number of programs and evaluations based on the following criteria: (1) we included programs that received federal funding in fiscal year 2012 and are continuing operations as of May 2013 and (2) for each focus area, we chose programs with the most recent evaluations and included up to two of the most recent studies for those programs. Some agencies provided us with performance reviews and other reports containing performance measurements that we did not include in our review of evaluations. When drafting our report, we provided agency officials with information on the studies to be included. We determined focus areas for implemented programs based on agency information about the purposes and goals of those programs. We also interviewed officials from departments, agencies, and program offices with authorized funding under the COMPETES Acts, including representatives from NSF's Education and Human Resources Directorate, Engineering Directorate, and Office of Integrative Activities; Energy's Science and ARPA-E; Commerce's NIST and Economic Development Administration; and Education's Office of Postsecondary Education.

We conducted this performance audit from October 2012 to July 2013 in accordance with generally accepted government auditing standards. Those standards require that we plan and perform the audit to obtain sufficient, appropriate evidence to provide a reasonable basis for our findings and conclusions based on our audit objectives. We believe that the evidence obtained provides a reasonable basis for our findings and conclusions based on our audit objectives.

---

[2]For GAO's definition of program evaluation, see GAO, *Designing Evaluations: 2012 Revision,* GAO-12-208G (Washington, D.C.: January, 2012).

Appendix II: Programs for Which the COMPETES Acts Specifically Authorized Funding

Figure 4 below shows the 40 programs for which the America Creating Opportunities to Meaningfully Promote Excellence in Technology, Education, and Science (COMPETES) Act of 2007 or the COMPETES Reauthorization Act of 2010 specifically authorized funding.

Figure 4: Programs for Which the America Creating Opportunities to Meaningfully Promote Excellence in Technology, Education, and Science (COMPETES) Act of 2007 or the COMPETES Reauthorization Act of 2010 Specifically Authorized Funding, by Agency

Programs	Origin			Funding		Current status			Focus areas of implemented programs				
	Existed before COMPETES	New under COMPETES '07	New under COMPETES '10	Funded[a]	Not funded	Repealed by COMPETES '10	No FY 12[b] appropriations	Currently operating	Research and development	Manufacturing performance	STEM[c] teacher training	STEM undergraduate	STEM graduate
COMMERCE — NIST[d]													
Federal Loan Guarantees for Innovative Technologies in Manufacturing		•	•			Agency is working toward implementation							
Loan Guarantees for Science Park Infrastructure		•	•			Agency is working toward implementation							
Regional Innovation Program		•		•									
Baldrige Performance Excellence Program[e]	•			•			•	•	•				
Hollings Manufacturing Extension Partnership	•			•				•	•				
NIST Green Jobs Act of 2010			•	•									
Technology Innovation Program		•		•			•		•				
EDUCATION													
Advanced Placement & International Baccalaureate Programs	•			•									
Alignment of Secondary School Graduation Requirements with the Demands of 21st Century Postsecondary Endeavors and Support for P-16 Education Data Systems	•			•									
Foreign Language Partnership Program	•			•	•								
Math Now for Elementary and Middle School Students Program	•			•	•								
Math Skills for Secondary School Students	•			•	•								
Mathematics and Science Partnership Bonus Grants	•			•	•								
Promising Practices in STEM Teaching	•			•	•								
Summer Term Education Program	•			•	•								
Teachers for a Competitive Tomorrow (bachelor's and master's programs)	•		•				•					•	
ENERGY													
Advanced Research Projects Agency–Energy	•		•					•	•				
Hydrocarbon Systems Science Talent Expansion	•			•									
National Energy Education Development	•			•	•								
Nuclear Science Talent Expansion Program	•			•									

☐ Subagency or office   ☐ Not applicable

		Origin			Funding		Current status			Focus areas of implemented programs				
	Programs	Existed before COMPETES	New under COMPETES '07	New under COMPETES '10	Funded[a]	Not funded	Repealed by COMPETES '10	No FY 12[b] appropriations	Currently operating	Research and development	Manufacturing performance	STEM[c] teacher training	STEM undergraduate	STEM graduate
ENERGY / Science[f]	Discovery Science and Engineering Innovation Institutes		•		•									
	Distinguished Scientist Program		•		•									
	Early Career Awards for Science, Engineering, and Math Researchers		•		•									
	Experiential-Based Learning Opportunities		•		•	•								
	Protecting America's Competitive Edge		•		•									
	Pilot Program of Grants to Specialty Schools for Science and Mathematics		•		•	•								
	Summer Institutes		•		•									
NATIONAL SCIENCE FOUNDATION	Advanced Technological Education	•			•				•				•	
	Experimental Program to Stimulate Competitive Research	•			•				•	•				
	Faculty Early Career Development Program	•			•				•	•				
	Graduate Research Fellowship Program	•			•				•					•
	Integrative Graduate Education and Research Traineeship	•			•				•					•
	Laboratory Science Pilot Program		•		•									
	Math and Science Education Partnerships	•			•				•			•		
	Major Research Instrumentation Program	•			•				•	•				
	Research Experiences for Undergraduates	•			•				•				•	
	Robert Noyce Teacher Scholarship Program	•			•				•			•		
	Science Master's Program		•		•			•						•
	STEM Talent Expansion Program	•			•				•				•	
	STEM Training Grant Program			•	•									
Total		12	23	5	18	22	9	3	13	4	3	3	3	3

Subagency or office Not applicable

Sources: GAO analysis of data from Congressional Research Service reports and relevant federal agencies.

[a]Programs were funded in at least one fiscal year from fiscal year 2008 through fiscal year 2012.

[b]FY refers to fiscal year.

[c]STEM refers to Science, Technology, Engineering, and Mathematics.

[d]NIST refers to National Institute of Standards and Technology.

[e]The Baldrige Performance Excellence Program did not receive federal funding in fiscal year 2012, but continues to operate with private funding.

[f]Science refers to the Office of Science.

Appendix III: Comments from the Department of Commerce

Note: Page numbers in draft report may differ from those in this report. GAO comments supplementing those in the report text appear at the end of this appendix.

UNITED STATES DEPARTMENT OF COMMERCE
The Secretary of Commerce
Washington, D.C. 20230

July 1, 2013

Ms. Karla Springer
Assistant Director
U.S. Government Accountability Office
441 G Street NW
Washington, DC 20548

Dear Ms. Springer:

The Department of Commerce (Department) and the National Institute of Standards and Technology (NIST) appreciate the opportunity to review and comment on the draft U.S. Government Accountability Office report entitled, "America COMPETES Acts: Overall Appropriations Have Increased and Have Mainly Funded Existing Research Entities."

The support for NIST's programs provided by these Acts has been invaluable in strengthening the innovative capacity of the United States and furthering the mission of the Department. The COMPETES Acts have played a significant role in strengthening and expanding NIST's abilities to fulfill its mission and address critical national challenges in the multiple fields, including manufacturing, cybersecurity, and healthcare.

Attached for your consideration are our consolidated comments on this report. If you have any questions, please contact me or Jim Stowers, Deputy Assistant Secretary for Legislative and Intergovernmental Affairs, at (202) 482-3663.

Sincerely,

Penny Pritzker

Enclosure

See comment 1.

**Department of Commerce Consolidated Comments on
GAO's Draft Report on America COMPETES Acts (GAO-13-612)**

The Department of Commerce (Department) has reviewed the draft GAO report entitled, "America COMPETES Acts: Overall Appropriations Have Increased and Have Mainly Funded Existing Research Entities" and appreciates the opportunity to comment on the content of the draft report. The draft report focuses only on programs that were specifically authorized in either the America COMPETES Act of 2007, or the America COMPETES Reauthorization Act of 2010 (the COMPETES Acts), which, for the Department's National Institute of Standards and Technology (NIST), include the Baldrige Performance Excellence Program (BPEP), the Hollings Manufacturing Extension Partnership Program (MEP), and the Technology Innovation Program (TIP). While these are or have been important programs for NIST, the Department considers that, as scoped, the draft report does not fully capture the significant positive impact that the COMPETES Acts have had on NIST.

In addition to the three specific extramural programs discussed in the report, the COMPETES Acts have provided critical support for NIST's core Laboratory Programs. The NIST Laboratory Programs work at the frontiers of measurement science to ensure that the U.S. system of measurements is firmly grounded on sound scientific and technical principles. NIST Laboratories address increasingly complex measurement challenges, ranging from the very small (nanoscale devices) to the very large (vehicles and buildings), and from the physical (renewable energy sources) to the virtual (cybersecurity and cloud computing). As new technologies develop and evolve, NIST's measurement research and services remain central to innovation, productivity, trade, and public safety.

The NIST Laboratory Programs provide industry, academia, and other federal agencies with:

- Scientific underpinnings for basic and derived measurement units, international standards, measurement and calibration services, and certified reference materials;

- Impartial expertise and leadership in basic and applied research to enable development of test methods and verified data to support the efficient commercialization and exchange of goods and services in industry and commerce;

- Expertise and support for the development of consensus-based standards and specifications that define technical and performance requirements for goods and services, with associated measurements and test methods for conformity; and

- Unique, cutting-edge User Facilities that support innovation in materials science, nanotechnology discovery and fabrication, and other emerging technology areas through the NIST Center for Neutron Research, which provides world-class neutron measurement capabilities to the U.S. research community, and the NIST Center for Nanoscale Science and Technology, which supports nanotechnology development from discovery to production.

The COMPETES Acts have played a significant role in strengthening and expanding NIST's abilities to fulfill its core mission responsibilities, and to address critical national challenges in multiple fields, including manufacturing, cybersecurity, and healthcare.

Specific Comments:

Page 11 – Footnote 9 states: "NIST's previously existing Baldrige Performance Excellence Program did not receive appropriations in fiscal year 2012 but is currently operating using private funds, according to agency officials." The Department wishes to emphasize that the Baldrige Performance Excellence Program (BPEP) remains an authorized program and operates as a key component of NIST's unique portfolio of programs that strengthen U.S. innovation and economic competitiveness. While BPEP did not receive appropriated funding in either FY 2012 or 2013, NIST's activities through BPEP have been supported by a significant, on-going, multi-year gift from the Baldrige Foundation, reflecting the intent and spirit of BPEP's authorizing legislation, the Malcolm Baldrige National Quality Improvement Act of 1987 (Pub. Law 100-107; 15 U.S.C. § 3711a, as amended). Accordingly, NIST suggests the following, more complete, footnote 9 statement: "NIST's Baldrige Performance Excellence Program (BPEP) did not receive appropriations in FY 2012 or 2013. According to agency officials, however, BPEP remains an important operating component of NIST's unique portfolio of programs that strengthen U.S. innovation and economic competitiveness. BPEP activities in FY 2012 and 2013 were supported by a significant, and on-going, multi-year gift from the Baldrige Foundation."

Page 16 – The section under the heading "Manufacturing performance" references (in footnote 16) an FY 2009 MEP Client Impact survey for the following Draft GAO Report statement: "A survey of MEP clients found that, for some clients, the program was successful in generating positive results measured in terms of sales, investment levels, cost savings, and jobs created or retained." It is pointed out that the draft report does not reference the most recent MEP Client Impact survey, to which NIST had previously directed GAO staff. These most recent survey results can be found at: http://www.nist.gov/mep/upload/MEP-Measuring-Results-Mar13-v2.pdf. NIST accordingly urges that the following be added to this section: "The most recent MEP Client Impact survey results[1] found that over FY 2011 and 2012, the average new and retained sales per client as a result of MEP services were $1.1M, the average cost savings per client were $161,000, the average new investment per client was $321,000, and an average of nine jobs were created and retained per client. Assuming the base funding of $125M over FY 2011 and 2012, the program's return on investment (ROI) ratios, based on client-reported impact, included total sales ROI of 118:1, cost savings ROI of 18:1, and client investment ROI of 35:1. MEP has created *or* retained a job for every $1,028 of federal investment, and has created a new job for every $3,357 of federal investment." In addition, NIST notes that a recent study, not referenced in the draft report, that benchmarked the small manufacturing programs of different countries, found that the U.S. ROI was significantly higher than that of the similar

See comment 2.

See comment 3.

See comment 4.

---

[1] Hollings Manufacturing Extension Partnership, *Delivering Measurable Results to Manufacturing Clients: Fiscal Year 2011 Results* (Washington, D.C.: March, 2013).

See comment 5.

programs of most other nations, despite the fact that the MEP program is funded at a level nearly $1/30^{th}$ of that of similar programs in Japan and $1/20^{th}$ of that of similar programs in Germany.[2]

Page 24 – Figure 4 on page 24 does not clearly communicate the authorization of funding for TIP or its current status. While funding for TIP was authorized in the America COMPETES Act of 2007, the America COMPETES Reauthorization Act of 2010 did not specifically authorize funding for TIP. Furthermore, in contrast to the BPEP, which has not been eliminated, FY 2012 saw the elimination of the TIP program. Therefore, the draft report should note for clarity that TIP did not receive federal appropriations in FY 2012, that NIST is in the process of winding down TIP program operations, and that agency officials expect that by FY 2014, all TIP awards will be closed out and all associated staff positions will be eliminated.

---

[2] Ezell and Atkinson, Information Technology and Innovation Foundation, International Benchmarking of Countries Policies and Programs Supporting SME Manufacturers (study prepared for the Hollings Manufacturing Extension Partnership, September, 2011.)

The following are GAO's comments on the National Institute of Standards and Technology's (NIST) letter, dated July 1, 2013.

GAO Comments

1. The scope of our review is based on a mandate in the America COMPETES Reauthorization Act of 2010 (COMPETES 2010) that calls for GAO to evaluate the extent to which programs authorized under the law have been funded, implemented, and are contributing to achieving the goals of the act. Our report addresses the total appropriations to NIST in fiscal years 2008 through 2012 in our first objective. To satisfy the needs of our congressional clients, we focused our review on programs for which COMPETES 2010 and the America Creating Opportunities to Meaningfully Promote Excellence in Technology, Education, and Science Act of 2007 (COMPETES 2007) specifically authorized funding.

2. Our draft report notes that the Baldrige Performance Excellence Program is currently operating using private funds, according to agency officials. We clarified in our footnote that the program remains authorized to receive funding. We did not include information about funding for fiscal year 2013 because that is beyond the scope of our review.

3. The scope of our review includes program evaluations published from 2008 through 2012. The draft report includes the findings from the Manufacturing Extension Partnership's (MEP) fiscal year 2009 client impact survey, which was the most recent survey published in our time frame. The results of the MEP 2011 client impact survey, which was published in March 2013, were outside the scope of our review.

4. To identify the evaluations we included in our analysis, as described in appendix I, we conducted a literature search and asked the agencies to provide evaluations of the programs that were published from 2008 through 2012. We conducted an initial review of the summaries of the reports or publications identified and excluded those that did not appear to evaluate how well programs were working. Based on the summary of the publication cited in NIST's letter, we concluded it was not in our scope, and it was not included in the selection of studies we reported on. When drafting our report, we provided agency officials with information on the studies to be included, and Commerce officials did not bring this publication to our attention at that time. However, upon receiving NIST's comments, we reviewed our criteria for identifying studies, and we continue to believe that our approach to identifying and selecting studies was appropriate.

5. We believe figure 4 clearly communicates the authorization of funding
   for the Technology Innovation Program (TIP) under COMPETES
   2007. Figure 4 also shows that TIP did not receive appropriations in
   fiscal year 2012, and that the program is not currently operating.
   Further, in the body of our report, we say that according to agency
   officials TIP is in the process of shutting down. We do not provide
   information about fiscal year 2014 because that is outside the scope
   of our review.

Appendix IV: GAO Contact and Staff Acknowledgments

GAO Contact	Frank Rusco, (202) 512-3841 or ruscof@gao.gov
Staff Acknowledgments	In addition to the individual named above, Karla Springer (Assistant Director), Nicole Dery, Cindy Gilbert, Michael Kendix, Cynthia Norris, Marietta Mayfield Revesz, and Barbara Timmerman made key contributions to this report.

GAO's Mission	The Government Accountability Office, the audit, evaluation, and investigative arm of Congress, exists to support Congress in meeting its constitutional responsibilities and to help improve the performance and accountability of the federal government for the American people. GAO examines the use of public funds; evaluates federal programs and policies; and provides analyses, recommendations, and other assistance to help Congress make informed oversight, policy, and funding decisions. GAO's commitment to good government is reflected in its core values of accountability, integrity, and reliability.
Obtaining Copies of GAO Reports and Testimony	The fastest and easiest way to obtain copies of GAO documents at no cost is through GAO's website (http://www.gao.gov). Each weekday afternoon, GAO posts on its website newly released reports, testimony, and correspondence. To have GAO e-mail you a list of newly posted products, go to http://www.gao.gov and select "E-mail Updates."
Order by Phone	The price of each GAO publication reflects GAO's actual cost of production and distribution and depends on the number of pages in the publication and whether the publication is printed in color or black and white. Pricing and ordering information is posted on GAO's website, http://www.gao.gov/ordering.htm. Place orders by calling (202) 512-6000, toll free (866) 801-7077, or TDD (202) 512-2537. Orders may be paid for using American Express, Discover Card, MasterCard, Visa, check, or money order. Call for additional information.
Connect with GAO	Connect with GAO on Facebook, Flickr, Twitter, and YouTube. Subscribe to our RSS Feeds or E-mail Updates. Listen to our Podcasts. Visit GAO on the web at www.gao.gov.
To Report Fraud, Waste, and Abuse in Federal Programs	Contact: Website: http://www.gao.gov/fraudnet/fraudnet.htm E-mail: fraudnet@gao.gov Automated answering system: (800) 424-5454 or (202) 512-7470
Congressional Relations	Katherine Siggerud, Managing Director, siggerudk@gao.gov, (202) 512-4400, U.S. Government Accountability Office, 441 G Street NW, Room 7125, Washington, DC 20548
Public Affairs	Chuck Young, Managing Director, youngc1@gao.gov, (202) 512-4800 U.S. Government Accountability Office, 441 G Street NW, Room 7149 Washington, DC 20548